Book 1
Facebook Social Power
BY SAM KEY

&

Book 2
MYSQL Programming Professional Made Easy
BY SAM KEY

Book 1
Facebook Social Power
BY SAM KEY

The Most Powerful Represented Facebook Guide to Making Money on anything on the Planet!

Programming Box Set #87: Facebook Social Power & MySQL Programming Professional Made Easy

Programming Box Set #87: Facebook Social Power & MySQL Programming Professional Made Easy

Table Of Contents

Introduction

I want to thank you and congratulate you for purchasing the book, "Learning the Social Power of Facebook: The Most Powerful Represented Facebook Guide to Making Money on anything on the Planet!"

This book contains proven steps and strategies on how to learn ways to use Facebook as a means to generate money for whatever business you have.

As you well may know by now, Facebook can be an amazing tool to promote your business, and of course, make money from it. However, not everyone knows how to do it, but with the help of this book, you'll learn everything you need to know about how to use Facebook to attract people's attention, and be successful in the world of business.

What are you waiting for? Start reading this book now and make money through Facebook as soon as possible!

Thanks again for purchasing this book, I hope you enjoy it!

Chapter 1: Make Use of Advertising based on E-Commerce

Because of Facebook's Ad Platform, a lot of marketers have been able to reach a wide range of audience because they get to put ads on their Facebook Pages that takes those who click the links to E-Commerce sites, so just the fact that these people get to see their pages already add a lot of traffic to their sites, and may allow people to get paid.

Oftentimes, people overlook the ads-to-direct sites but knowing how to go forth with it is very beneficial because it has a three-way approach that will help you earn a lot of money. Basically, this approach goes as follows:

FB Ads—Discount Pages/Website Sales—Buyers/Customers

One example of a company that benefited a lot from E-Commerce based Advertising through Facebook is Vamplets.com. Vamplets.com is popular for selling plush dolls—but these dolls aren't just regular plush dolls, as they are Vampire Plushies. When Vamplets used this kind of advertising, they were able to achieve 300% ROI, which is definitely a mean feat.

So, how then are you going to be able to use E-Commerce based Advertising for your business? Follow the pointers below and you'll understand how.

Choose your Audience

First and foremost, you have to choose your target demographic so that sales funnel will be easier to be filled. Facebook will allow you to choose between one of the following:

- Custom Audience from Your Website
- Custom Audience from MailChimp
- Data File Custom Audience
- Custom Audience from Your Mobile App

Once you're able to choose your target demographic, it will be easy for you to convert an ad to money because these people will be interested in what you have to offer because you're no longer going to be generalizing things.

You can also choose your audience via the Facebook Audience Insights Category. Here, you'll be able to find people who are interested in your campaign, based on pages that they have liked, so that you'd know that they would like to see what your business is all about. This is called interest-based campaigning.

You can also try using Lookalike Audiences. You can do this by making use of your existing audience, and then pick the next group of people who act and feel similar to your original audience so your posts would be able to reach more people, and you'd get more traffic and revenue, as well. It would be nice to test audiences, too, so you'd know who's interested in your services.

For example, you're selling clothes for pregnant women. You really cannot expect people who are single or who are still in High School click your ads, or like your page, because of course, they're not in that stage of their lives yet. So, make sure that you choose audiences that you know will listen to what you have to say.

Then, go on and place a Facebook Pixel to the footer of your page, and your ads will then be connected to Facebook. You can also choose to send traffic to one audience group this week, then to another group the next.

Make Proper Segments for Visitors of Your Homepage

Of course, you have to make sure that your homepage gets the attention of many because if it doesn't, and if people feel alienated by it, you also cannot expect that you'll gain profit from it. The three basic things that you have to have in your homepage include:

- New Sales Items
- Branding Ads
- Other Promotional Ads

Make Segments for Categories and Products

You can also place ads in various categories of your website so that even if your customer does not check out all the items he placed in the cart, your website will still gain some revenue because more often than not, customers like to buy products based on ads that were able to get through to them.

Chapter 2: Use Fan Marketing E-Commerce

Basically, Fan Marketing E-Commerce is the means of promoting your business by making sure that you post ads through your page and have those ads appear on the newsfeeds of your target demographic.

Research has it that fans become more interested in a new product or business when they see ads, instead of when they learn about the said products through contests or just from other people. Why? Simply because ads are more professional ways of getting people's attention and marketing products, and Facebook definitely makes that easy.

However, it's not enough that you just have a fanpage. You have to make sure that you actually use the said page and that it doesn't get stuck. You can do this by making sure that you constantly post a thing or two, and that you interact with your fans, as well.

You see, a study held in 2011 showed that although over a hundred thousand people may like a certain page, sometimes, revenue only gets up by 7%, because the owners of the fan pages do not interact with their fans and have not posted anything in a while. You also have to make sure that you stay relevant by being able to attract new fans from time to time.

Once you do this right, you'll be able to create the process of:

FB Ads—FB Fans—See Posts—Click to Website—Buyers/Customers

Some of those who have greatly benefited from Fan Marketing Strategies include:

- Baseball Roses, a company that sells artificial roses made from old baseball balls, who gained over 437% of ROI with the help of Facebook Fan Marketing;
- Superherostuff.com, a website that sells merchandise based on famous superheroes, such as t-shirts, jackets, hoodies, shoes, and more, gained over 150% ROI, and;

- Rosehall Kennel Breeds, a company that specializes in selling German Shepherds, gained over a whopping 4,000% of ROI for its fan acquisition speed alone—and that's definitely something that should inspire you.

So, what exactly did these companies do and how did they make use of Facebook Fan Marketing E-Commerce for their own benefit? Here are some tips that you can follow:

1. **Make sure that you post a new update after your last update is gone from people's newsfeeds.** Sometimes, you see posts in your feed for even a day or two after posting, but there are also times when they are gone after just a couple of minutes or hours. It actually varies due to how fans see or react on those posts and Facebook's EdgeRank Algorithm will be able to give you a glimpse of how your post is doing, based on three main factors, which are:

    a. **Likes per Post.** You'd know that people are interested in your posts when they actually make it a point to like the said posts, and it's great because likes are always updated in real time, and will also let your posts stay longer on people's newsfeeds. Therefore, make sure to check the numbers of likes regularly.

    b. **Comments per Post.** Comments are always time-stamped, but you cannot always rely on these as not everyone like to comment on posts, and you cannot define whether the posts appear on people's feeds, or they're simply too lazy to comment.

    c. **Impressions per Post.** This is basically the number of times a single status has been viewed. While the numbers update as more and more people get to see your post, there are also times when the number stay stagnant only because Facebook refuses to update, so may have to wait a while to see the real numbers.

    A good way of trying to gauge your influence on Facebook is by posting an hourly status, then make sure that you record the number of likes, comments, and impressions, and then record the data on Excel. Make a graph, then see the ratio of how much your posts appear on one's feeds, and decide the average number of posts that you have to do per day or per week.

2. **Make sure that the things you post are not redundant.** People these days have really short attention span so it would be nice if you know how to post varied content. Make sure that your fans have something to come back to each day, and that they don't get bored with whatever it is that you have on your website and won't click the "dislike" button.

3. **Do some marketing.** Again, you're trying to make money by means of promoting your products so you have to do a lot of marketing via Facebook. An easy way of doing this is by giving your fans discount codes that they can use if they're interested in buying your products so that they'd constantly check your page.

4. **Make sure that social sharing buttons are open.** While you may use Facebook as the original platform for advertising your services, you also have to realize that it's important to share your content on other websites or social networking sites so that more people would get to see what you have to offer. Also, make sure that your page is set to public because you really cannot expect people to know what you want them to know if your page is set to private. When your page is public, they'll be able to like, comment, and share your posts, which will bring you more traffic and more revenue. Then, connect your Facebook Page to your other social media accounts so that whenever you post updates on your Facebook Page, the updates will be sent to all your other accounts, as well.

5. **Don't ever try hard-selling tactics.** It's always better to be subtle because people hate it when they feel like their feeds are full of pages that just sell their products outright without making the fans understand what they're all about. So, try asking your fans some questions, or create polls about what kind of products or services they like but never just put up ads or ask them to "buy your products" right away without helping them know that you're their "friend" and that you want them to know what's best in the market right now. You can also place behind the scenes videos of what goes on in your company, or

post testimonials from past customers to get the curiosity of your fans running. This way, you get to be trustworthy and your business will be more authoritative, and people would be more interested.

6. **And, make sure that you provide good customer service.** For a Facebook Page to be successful, it doesn't have to be bombarded with ads, you also have to make sure that you get to be friends with your customers and that loyalty and trust are built. For example, when one of your fans posts questions or queries on your page, take time to answer the said questions, and make sure that you reply as soon as possible so that you get to create some sense of urgency and that people will know that you're there.

Keep these tips in mind and you'll surely be able to make use of your Facebook Page to give you a lot of profit. Oh, and make sure to have ample amounts of patience, too!

Chapter 3: Connect Facebook Ads to E-Mail

Another way of making use of Facebook to gain revenue is by connecting ads to e-mails. Basically, it's a way of promoting content to your e-mail subscribers so that it will be easier for your fans to know about your new products or services, or to know if there are contests or events coming up based on the updates that you have sent.

Basically, when Facebook ads are sent to people's e-mails, there are more chances of acquiring a larger number of future subscribers. And Facebook makes this easy for you as they have a feature that allows you to add E-mail lists to your Fan Page so that whenever you post an update, your e-mail list will automatically get to know it, too.

The target formula is as follows:

FB Ad—Squeeze—E-mail Sign Up—E-mail Open—E-mail Click to Visit—Buyers/Customers

So, in order for you to be successful in this kind of marketing tactic, you first have to get a target demographic of e-mail subscribers. While it may be easy to just post an invite so your fans would want to be part of your e-mail list, it will be nice to filter people who probably won't open your e-mails and choose people who would be interested in what you have to offer. You can do this by adding information to the Facebook Ad Copy Page. The information that you need are as follows:

- Gender
- Age
- Location
- Interests
- Relationship Status
- Educational Attainment/Level
- Workplace
- Pages that have been liked (So you'd get to see if they would like the posts that you'd be making)

Then, go on and upload the e-mail list on your Facebook Page by giving Facebook a list of e-mails from MailChimp or any other AutoResponder Service, so that the e-mail addresses of your fans will be synchronized to your page.

Effective Message Integration

It's so easy to send a message but it's never really easy to make sure that those messages are effective. However, there are a couple of tips that you can keep in mind:

- Optimize Facebook Ad Headlines with Catchy Subject Lines so that your fans will be interested to open your e-mails. Examples include:
    - Do Gamers dream of DOTA II?
    - Why your 12 year old likes Miley Cyrus
    - 8 Most Annoying Social Media Moments of 2014
    - 3 Ways to Improve Your Life

  Basically, you have to make sure that your subject lines have a lot to do with your content and with your line of business so that your fans won't be confused and they'd be interested in what you have to say.

- Add your fans' testimonials and comments about your services so others would know that you are for real.
- Add images into your e-mails. After all, people have short attention span and they would appreciate it if they get to see images as part of your e-mails because these would get their attention more and would help them picture what you are talking about.
- Let your fans know that you are going to send another e-mail blast by updating your Facebook status.
- Tease some of the contents of your e-mail on your status updates so that your fans will be hyped up and will be curious to open their e-mails.

- Make use of Facebook Landing Tabs, and Social Log-in Software, so that whenever your fans open their e-mails, it will automatically add traffic to your Facebook Page, and your website, as well.
- Put some sort of disclaimer, or a line that allows your fans to unsubscribe if they want to, because they have to know that you're not actually forcing them to read your messages and that they have the choice to unsubscribe from your list.
- And don't forget to send Thank You messages. If you want to foster a great relationship with your fans, you have to let them know that you're thankful that they're around, and that they're part of your list, so that they will realize that it's substantial to read the content that you are sending, and that it's important to be a fan of yours, instead of just talking about yourself all the time, without thinking of your fans. After all, without them, you won't gain any profit so you have to be grateful that they're around.

You can also run Geo-targeted ads, or ads that are meant for people who live in one location alone, so that the e-mails would feel more personal and so that your fans will know that you are really thinking of them. Sometimes, targeting people who are in the same vicinity as you is more effective because you get to really connect with them as you experience the same things and you'd know that they are more likely to try your products, unlike those that live in far away places.

If you're able to be successful with Facebook E-mail marketing, you can definitely gain more traffic and more revenue. One of those Fortune 500 Companies actually gained 400% ROI just because of its e-mail subscribers, so you can expect that you'll gain more, too, but only if you follow the tips given above. Good Luck!

Chapter 4: Making Use of Your Ad-Supported Sites

Ad-Supported sites are those that run advertisements and allow the said ads to be shared to your Facebook Page.

This is especially helpful for those whose businesses are really situated online, and those whose blogs or websites are their bread and butter. So, if that's the case, it would be important to create a Facebook Page that's connected to your blog or your website so that things would be formalized more. People like it when they see that a certain website has a Facebook Page because they feel like they'd get to be updated more without having to go to the website.

The formula for this is as follows:

FB Ad—FB Fan—See Post—Click to Website—Click Ad

So basically, when people click ads on your website that take them to your Facebook Page and Vice Versa, you not only gain traffic, you get to be paid, as well. This is similar as the popular Pay-Per-Click Advertising tactic. And also, when you get more fans from various parts of the world, your revenue will increase even more mainly because your content now gets to reach a large number of people, which evidently is beneficial for your business.

Proud Single Moms, a site targeted to help single mothers, gained over $5,000 for Facebook Ads alone that were promoted on their Facebook Page that has around 100,000 fans. On their blog, they made sure that they posted topics that single mothers would be able to relate to, and they also made sure that they used keywords that would give them high search rank on search engines such as Google, or Yahoo.

You can make use of Keyword Tools that are found online to find the perfect keywords that are related to your niche. Once you use these keywords in your posts, you'll be able to generate traffic and revenue.

The main reason why ads on Facebook are so effective is the fact that almost everyone in the world has a Facebook account, so of course, you can expect them to see your posts and the ads that are on your page, too. Plus, when you post links of your blog's content to your Facebook Page, there are more chances that people will get to read these posts because of course, they found it on Facebook, and they didn't use the web just so they could see your website. And these days, that is very important. The key is to be reachable.

Proud Single Moms made sure that they posted the links of blog post updates each day and in just a matter of six months, they were able to create another website that gave them more revenue.

Chapter 5: Other Tips

Aside from the techniques given above, you can also make use of these Facebook Marketing tactics to make sure that your business gains more profit:

Ads through SMS

While it may not be as popular as other Facebook Marketing tips, the combination of Facebook Ads and Text Messaging have slowly been gaining the attention of many for being a fast-paced approach when it comes to advertising products and services. In fact, around 24% of marketers on mobile have gained more ROI just because people have responded to text messages regarding product promotions, and have tried the coupons that they gave away through text, too.

This is especially effective for those with business that are related to food as free coupons that were sent to Facebook fans helped these fans to be more interested to try certain products that were being sold, and have visited the restaurants more often in hopes that they'd be given more information and more freebies, too. When people feel like they know the latest news about a certain establishment or a certain product, it's easy for them to appreciate the said establishment and so they get to patronize it more. This then gave the restaurants around $60,000 more revenue, which is definitely something good!

Give Some Offers that they won't be able to refuse!

Mostly everyone want freebies, because money is really hard to come by these days and not everything is affordable, so of course, they feel like it's nice to be able to get some goodies or services for free. Facebook Offers actually help you create deals with your fans that are not available on other social media platforms.

Basically, you ask your customers to like your page and leave their e-mail addresses so that you can send them coupons or offers that they can redeem in your store. First, make the offers exclusive to your fans then when it gets successful, you can then make more offers for people outside your circle so that more people would be excited to try your products and see what you have to offer.

Don't think about losing profit. More often than not, when you give things away for free, people will be more interested to try your other products and so of course, they'd be paying you in the future, so it's like you have made them your investment and soon enough, you'll benefit from them.

Create Apps for them

A lot of people these days rely on apps that they could use to open certain websites or pages, and of course, if you create an app for your business, it will be easy for them to read your content and it will be easy for you to reach them. They wouldn't have to deal with the hassle of using the browser just so they could see some offers or read articles connected to a certain topic that they would like to learn about. Also, it's better if you add links to your Facebook Page to the app that you have created so that everything will be merged together.

You can also create Facebook Ads without creating a Facebook Page

You can do this by selecting the Clicks to Website option of Facebook or the Website Conversions tab. People will still get to see your ads on the right side of their pages. You know, those ads that appear near the chat sidebar, so in a way, you still get to promote your business, but having Facebook Pages are still way better because then the ads appear on the main feeds and not just on the right side tabs.

Create a catchy headline

Just like how important it is to create effective e-mail subject lines, it's also important to create catchy ad headlines because these will attract people's attention and will allow people to understand what you and your business are all about.

The rule of thumb is to make sure that the headline of your ad is the same as the title of your page so it will be easily recognizable. It would also be helpful if you pair it up with an image that you have created so that people will be able to connect the said image to your business and it will be easy for them to remember your ad.

Make use of Sponsored Stories, too

You see, sponsored stories are the results of how people interact on your page or how they appreciate your content. Basically, whenever someone likes your posts or updates, or when they comment on or share your content, it creates "Facebook Stories". To make sure that these stories appear on a lot of people's newsfeeds, you have to pay a minimal fee, so it's like you get to easily advertise your content and you make sure that people actually get to see them.

But make sure that you choose the best bidding and advertising options

What's good about Facebook is that it allows you to choose the best kind of bidding option that will be good for your business. For example, you can choose whether you want to gain revenue through clicks, or through impressions then you can then reach your objective after you have customized your bids.

You can also choose whether you'd like to pay for your content to be advertised by paying daily, or by paying for a lifetime. The advantages of paying for a lifetime is that you'd know that your content will always be published and that you'd basically have nothing else to worry about, but the thing is that when you want to change the products you are advertising or if you're going to close your business down, it's like you'll get people confused because they'll still see ads from your old site, and they'd keep looking for your services. So, it's recommended that you just pay for the ads daily or on a case to case basis, say there's an event that's coming up and the like, so that it won't be hard for you to reach your followers and gain potential fans in the process, too.

When making use of image ads, make sure that text is only 20%

You would not want to bombard your followers with too many texts and images in just one post. Plus, your image ads won't be approved if they contain more than 20% of text.

In order to know if your ads are following Facebook's guidelines, check out the Facebook Grid Tool that will help you see how your ad looks and what needs to be changed, if necessary.

Let others help you

Sometimes, two heads are better than one, and it's great because when you add another admin to your page, they can also update your page so whenever you're busy or if you cannot answer queries right away, these other admins can help you out.

Just make sure that you choose admins that you can trust and that they know a lot about your business so the things they will be posting will be substantial, too. To do this, just go to the Ad Manager option of Facebook, then click Ad Account Roles, and choose Add a User. Make sure that the person you will add as an admin is your friend on Facebook and that his e-mail address can easily be searched through Facebook, too.

And, don't forget to choose the revenue model that is right for you

To do this, you may have to try each technique first, but don't worry because sooner or later, you'll find the one that proves to be the most effective for your business.

In the marketing business, trial and error really is one of the biggest keys to success, so don't worry if you feel like you aren't being successful right away. Take chances and soon enough, you'll be on the path to success. Good Luck!

Conclusion

Thank you again for purchasing this book!

I hope this book was able to help you understand how you can use Facebook to advertise your business and gain lots of revenue.

The next step is to follow the techniques listed here, and don't be afraid to try each one because sooner or later, you'll find the perfect fit for you. Advertise through Facebook and let your business soar!

Thank you and good luck!

Book 2
MYSQL Programming Professional Made Easy

BY SAM KEY

Expert MYSQL Programming Language Success in a Day for any Computer User!

Table Of Contents

Introduction

I want to thank you and congratulate you for purchasing the book, “MYSQL Programming Professional Made Easy: Expert MYSQL Programming Language Success in a Day for any Computer User!”.

This book contains proven steps and strategies on how to manage MySQL databases.

The book will teach you the fundamentals of SQL and how to apply it on MySQL. It will cover the basic operations such as creating and deleting tables and databases. Also, it will tell you how to insert, update, and delete records in MySQL. In the last part of the book, you will be taught on how to connect to your MySQL server and send queries to your database using PHP.

Thankfully, by this time, this subject is probably a piece of cake for you since you might already have experienced coding in JavaScript and PHP, which are prerequisites to learning MySQL.

However, it does not mean that you will have a difficult time learning MySQL if you do not have any idea on those two scripting languages. In this book, you will learn about SQL, which works a bit different from programming languages.

Being knowledgeable alone with SQL can give you a solid idea on how MySQL and other RDBMS work. Anyway, thanks again for purchasing this book, I hope you enjoy it!

Chapter 1: Introduction to MySQL

This book will assume that you are already knowledgeable about PHP. It will focus on database application on the web. The examples here will use PHP as the main language to use to access a MySQL database. Also, this will be focused on Windows operating system users.

As of now, MySQL is the most popular database system by PHP programmers. Also, it is the most popular database system on the web. A few of the websites that use MySQL to store their data are Facebook, Wikipedia, and Twitter.

Commonly, MySQL databases are ran on web servers. Because of that, you need to use a server side scripting language to use it.

A few of the good points of MySQL against other database systems are it is scalable (it is good to use in small or large scale applications), fast, easy to use, and reliable. Also, if you are already familiar with SQL, you will not have any problems in manipulating MySQL databases.

Preparation

In the first part of this book, you will learn SQL or Standard Query Language. If you have a database program, such as Microsoft Access, installed in your computer, you can use it to practice and apply the statements you will learn.

In case you do not, you have two options. Your first option is to get a hosting account package that includes MySQL and PHP. If you do not want to spend tens of dollars for a paid web hosting account, you can opt for a free one. However, be informed that most of them will impose limitations or add annoyances, such as ads, in your account. Also, some of them have restrictions that will result to your account being banned once you break one of them.

Your second option is to get XAMMP, a web server solution that includes Apache, MySQL, and PHP. It will turn your computer into a local web server. And with it, you can play around with your MySQL database and the PHP codes you want to experiment with. Also, it comes with phpMyAdmin. A tool that will be discussed later in this book.

Chapter 2: Database and SQL

What is a database? A database is an application or a file wherein you can store data. It is used and included in almost all types of computer programs. A database is usually present in the background whether the program is a game, a word processor, or a website.

A database can be a storage location for a player's progress and setting on a game. It can be a storage location for dictionaries and preferences in word processors. And it can be a storage location for user accounts and page content in websites.

There are different types and forms of databases. A spreadsheet can be considered a database. Even a list of items in a text file can be considered one, too. However, unlike the database that most people know or familiar with, those kinds of databases are ideal for small applications.

RDBMS

The type of database that is commonly used for bigger applications is RDBMS or relational database management system. MySQL is an RDBMS. Other RDBMS that you might have heard about are Oracle database, Microsoft Access, and SQL Server.

Inside an RDBMS, there are tables that are composed of rows, columns, and indexes. Those tables are like spreadsheets. Each cell in a table holds a piece of data. Below is an example table:

id	*username*	*password*	*email*	*firstname*	*las am*
1	*Johnnyxxx*	*123abc*	*jjxxx@gmail.com*	*Johnny*	*Ste*
2	*cutiepatutie*	*qwertyuiop*	*cuteme@yahoo.com*	*Sara*	*Br h*

3	*masterm iller*	*theGear 12*	mgshades@g mail.com	*Maste r*	*Mille r*
4	*j_sasaki*	*H9fmaN Ca*	j_sasaki@gm ail.com	*Johnn y*	*Sasak i*

Note: this same table will be used as the main reference of all the examples in this book. Also, developers usually encrypt their passwords in their databases. They are not encrypted for the sake of an example.

In the table, which the book will refer to as the account table under the sample database, there are six columns (or fields) and they are id, username, password, email, firstname, and lastname. As of now, there are only four rows. Rows can be also called entries or records. Take note that the first row is not part of the count. They are just there to represent the name of the columns as headers.

An RDBMS table can contain one or more tables.

Compared to other types of databases, RDBMS are easier to use and manage because it comes with a standardized set of method when it comes to accessing and manipulating data. And that is SQL or Standard Query Language.

SQL

Before you start learning MySQL, you must familiarize yourself with SQL or Standard Query Language first. SQL is a language used to manipulate and access relational database management systems. It is not that complicated compared to learning programming languages.

Few of the things you can do with databases using SQL are:

- Get, add, update, and delete data from databases
- Create, modify, and delete databases
- Modify access permissions in databases

Most database programs use SQL as the standard method of accessing databases, but expect that some of them have a bit of variations. Some statements have different names or keywords while some have different methods to do things. Nevertheless, most of the usual operations are the same for most of them.

A few of the RDBMS that you can access using SQL – with little alterations – are MySQL, SQL Server, and Microsoft Access.

Chapter 3: SQL Syntax

SQL is like a programming language. It has its own set of keywords and syntax rules. Using SQL is like talking to the database. With SQL, you can pass on commands to the database in order for it to present and manipulate the data it contains for you. And you can do that by passing queries and statements to it.

SQL is commonly used interactively in databases. As soon as you send a query or statement, the database will process it immediately. You can perform some programming in SQL, too. However, it is much easier to leave the programming part to other programming languages. In the case of MySQL, it is typical that most of the programming is done with PHP, which is the most preferred language to use with it.

SQL's syntax is simple. Below is an example:

```
SELECT username FROM account
```

In the example, the query is commanding the database to get all the data under the username column from the account table. The database will reply with a recordset or a collection of records.

In MySQL, databases will also return the number of rows it fetched and the duration that it took to fetch the result.

Case Sensitivity

As you can see, the SQL query is straightforward and easy to understand. Also, take note that unlike PHP, MySQL is not case sensitive. Even if you change the keyword SELECT's case to select, it will still work. For example:

```
seLeCT username from account
```

However, as a standard practice, it is best that you type keywords on uppercase and values in lowercase.

Line Termination

In case that you will perform or send consecutive queries or a multiline query, you need to place a semicolon at the end of each statement to separate them. By the way, MySQL does not consider a line to be a statement when it sees a new line character – meaning, you can place other parts of your queries on multiple lines. For example:

```
SELECT

username

FROM

account;
```

New lines are treated like a typical whitespace (spaces and tabs) character. And the only accepted line terminator is a semicolon. In some cases, semicolons are not needed to terminate a line.

Chapter 4: SQL Keywords and Statements

When you memorize the SQL keywords, you can say that you are already know SQL or MySQL. Truth be told, you will be mostly using only a few SQL keywords for typical database management. And almost half of the queries you will be making will be SELECT queries since retrieving data is always the most used operation in databases.

Before you learn that, you must know how to create a database first.

CREATE DATABASE

Creating a database is simple. Follow the syntax below:

```
CREATE DATABASE <name of database>;
```

To create the sample database where the account table is located, this is all you need to type:

```
CREATE DATABASE sample;
```

Easy, right? However, an empty database is a useless database. You cannot enter any data to it yet since you do not have tables yet.

CREATE TABLE

Creating a table requires a bit of planning. Before you create a table, you must already know the columns you want to include in it. Also, you need to know the size, type, and other attributes of the pieces of data that you will insert on your columns. Once you do, follow the syntax below:

```
CREATE TABLE <name of table>

(

<name of column 1> <data type(size)> <attributes>,

<name of column 2> <data type(size)> <attributes>,
```

```
<name of column 3> <data type(size)> <attributes>
);
```

By the way, you cannot just create a table out of nowhere. To make sure that the table you will create will be inside a database, you must be connected to one. Connection to databases will be discussed in the later part of this book. As of now, imagine that you are now connected to the sample database that was just created in the previous section.

To create the sample account table, you need to do this:

```
CREATE TABLE account
(
id int(6) PRIMARY KEY UNSIGNED AUTO_INCREMENT PRIMARY KEY,
username varchar(16),
password varchar(16),
email varchar(32),
firstname var(16),
lastname var(16),
);
```

The example above commands the database to create a table named account. Inside the parentheses, the columns that will be created inside the account table are specified. They are separated with a comma. The first column that was created was the id column.

According to the example, the database needs to create the id column (id). It specified that the type of data that it will contain would be integers with six characters (int(6)). Also, it specified some optional attributes. It said that the id column will be the PRIMARY KEY of the table and its values will AUTO_INCREMENT – these will be discussed later. Also, it specified that the integers or data under it will be UNSIGNED, which means that only positive integers will be accepted.

MySQL Data Types

As mentioned before, databases or RDBMS accept multiple types of data. To make databases clean, it is required that you state the data type that you will input in your table's columns. Aside from that, an RDBMS also needs to know the size of the data that you will enter since it will need to allocate the space it needs to store the data you will put in it. Providing precise information about the size of your data will make your database run optimally.

Below are some of the data types that you will and can store in a MySQL database:

- INT(size) – integer data type. Numbers without fractional components or decimal places. A column with an INT data type can accept any number between -2147483648 to 2147483648. In case that you specified that it will be UNSIGNED, the column will accept any number between 0 to 4294967295. You can specify the number of digits with INT. The maximum is 11 digits – it will include the negative sign (-).
- FLOAT(size, decimal) – float data type. Numbers with fractional components or decimal places. It cannot be UNSIGNED. You can specify the number of digits it can handle and the number of decimal places it will store. If you did not specify the size and number of decimals, MySQL will set it to 10 digits and 2 decimal places (the decimal places is included in the count of the digits). Float can have the maximum of 24 digits.
- TIME – time will be stored and formatted as HH:MM:SS.
- DATE – date will be stored and formatted as YYYY-MM-DD. It will not accept any date before year 1,000. And it will not accept date that exceeds 31 days and 12 months.

- DATETIME – combination of DATE and TIME formatted as YYYY-MM-DD HH:MM:SS.
- TIMESTAMP – formatted differently from DATETIME. Its format is YYYYMMDDHHMMSS. It can only store date and time between 19700101000000 and 20371231235959 (not accurate).
- CHAR(size) – stores strings with fixed size. It can have a size of 1 to 255 characters. It uses static memory allocation, which makes it perform faster than VARCHAR. It performs faster because the database will just multiply its way to reach the location of the data you want instead of searching every byte to find the data that you need. To make the data fixed length, it is padded with spaces after the last character.
- VARCHAR(size) – stores strings with variable length size. It can have a size of 1 to 255 characters. It uses dynamic memory allocation, which is slower than static. However, when using VARCHAR, it is mandatory to specify the data's size.
- BLOB –store BLOBs (Binary Large Objects). Data is stored as byte strings instead of character strings (in contrast to TEXT). This makes it possible to store images, documents, or other files in the database.
- TEXT – store text with a length of 65535 characters or less.
- ENUM(x, y, z) – with this, you can specify the values that can be only stored.

INT, BLOB, and TEXT data types can be set smaller or bigger. For example, you can use TINYINT instead of INT to store smaller data. TINYINT can only hold values ranging from -128 to 127 compared to INT that holds values ranging from -2147483648 to 2147483647.

The size of the data type ranges from TINY, SMALL, MEDIUM, NORMAL, and BIG.

- TINYINT, SMALLINT, MEDIUMINT, INT, and BIGINT
- TINYBLOB, SMALLBLOB, MEDIUMBLOB, BLOB, and BIGBLOB

- TINYTEXT, SMALLTEXT, MEDIUMTEXT, TEXT, and BIGTEXT

You already know how to create databases and tables. Now, you need to learn how to insert values inside those tables.

INSERT INTO and VALUES

There are two ways to insert values in your database. Below is the syntax for the first method:

```
INSERT INTO <name of table>

VALUES (<value 1>, <value 2>, <value 3>);
```

The same result be done by:

```
INSERT INTO <name of table>

(<column 1>, <column 2>, <column 3>)

VALUES (<value 1>, <value 2>, <value 3>);
```

Take note that the first method will assign values according to the arrangement of your columns in the tables. In case you do not want to enter a data to one of the columns in your table, you will be forced to enter an empty value.

On the other hand, if you want full control of the INSERT operation, it will be much better to indicate the name of the corresponding columns that will be given data. Take note that the database will assign the values you will write with respect of the arrangement of the columns in your query.

For example, if you want to insert data in the example account table, you need to do this:

```
INSERT INTO account

(username, password, email, firstname, lastname)
```

VALUES

("Johnnyxxx", "123abc", "jjxxx@gmail.com, "Johnny", "Stew");

The statement will INSERT one entry to the database. You might have noticed that the example did not include a value for the ID field. You do not need to do that since the ID field has the AUTO_INCREMENT attribute. The database will be the one to generate a value to it.

SELECT and FROM

To check if the entry you sent was saved to the database, you can use SELECT. As mentioned before, the SELECT statement will retrieve all the data that you want from the database. Its syntax is:

SELECT <column 1> FROM <name of table>;

If you use this in the example account table and you want to get all the usernames in it, you can do it by:

SELECT username FROM account;

In case that you want to multiple records from two or more fields, you can do that by specifying another column. For example:

SELECT username, email FROM account;

WHERE

Unfortunately, using SELECT alone will provide you with tons of data. And you do not want that all the time. To filter out the results you want or to specify the data you want to receive, you can use the WHERE clause. For example:

SELECT <column 1> FROM <name of table>

```
WHERE <column> <operator> <value>;
```

If ever you need to get the username of all the people who have Johnny as their first name in the account table, you do that by:

```
SELECT username FROM account

WHERE firstname = “Johnny”;
```

In the query above, the database will search all the records in the username column that has the value Johnny on the firstname column. The query will return Johnnyxxx and j_sasaki.

LIMIT

What if you only need a specific number of records to be returned? You can use the LIMIT clause for that. For example:

```
SELECT <column 1> FROM <name of table>

LIMIT <number>;
```

If you only want one record from the email column to be returned when you use SELECT on the account table, you can do it by:

```
SELECT email FROM account

LIMIT 1;
```

You can the LIMIT clause together with the WHERE clause for you to have a more defined search. For example:

```
SELECT username FROM account

WHERE firstname = “Johnny”

LIMIT 1;
```

Instead of returning two usernames that have Johnny in the firstname field, it will only return one.

UPDATE and SET

What if you made a mistake and you want to append an entry on your table? Well, you can use UPDATE for that. For example:

UPDATE <name of table>

SET <column 1>=<value 1>, <column 1>=<value 1>, <column 1>=<value 1>

WHERE <column> <operator> <value>;

In the example account table, if you want to change the name of all the people named Master to a different one, you can do that by:

UPDATE account

SET firstname=”David”

WHERE firstname=”Master”;

Take note, you can perform an UPDATE without the WHERE clause. However, doing so will make the database think that you want to UPDATE all the records in the table. Remember that it is a bit complex to ROLLBACK changes in MySQL, so be careful.

DELETE

If you do not to remove an entire row, you can use DELETE. However, if you just want to delete or remove one piece of data in a column, it is better to use UPDATE and place a blank value instead. To perform a DELETE, follow this syntax:

DELETE FROM <name of table>

WHERE <column> <operator> <value>;

If you want to delete the first row in the account table, do this:

DELETE FROM account

WHERE id = 1;

Just like with the UPDATE statement, make sure that you use the WHERE clause when using DELETE. If not, all the rows in your table will disappear.

TRUNCATE TABLE

If you just want to remove all the data inside your table and keep all the settings that you have made to it you need to use TRUNCATE TABLE. This is the syntax for it:

TRUNCATE TABLE <name of table>;

If you want to do that to the account table, do this by entering:

TRUNCATE TABLE account;

DROP TABLE and DROP DATABASE

Finally, if you want to remove a table or database, you can use DROP. Below are examples on how to DROP the account table and sample database.

DROP TABLE account;

DROP DATABASE sample;

Chapter 5: MySQL and PHP

You already know how to manage a MySQL server to the most basic level. Now, it is time to use all those statements and use PHP to communicate with the MySQL server.

To interact or access a MySQL database, you need to send SQL queries to it. There are multiple ways you can do that. But if you want to do it in the web or your website, you will need to use a server side scripting language. And the best one to use is PHP.

In PHP, you can communicate to a MySQL server by using PDO (PHP Data Objects), MySQL extension, or MySQLi extension. Compared to MySQLi extension, PDO is a better choice when communicating with a MySQL database. However, in this book, only MySQLi extension will be discussed since it is less complex and easier to use.

Connecting to a MySQL database:

Before you can do or say anything to a MySQL server or a database, you will need to connect to it first. To do that, follow this example:

```
<?php
$dbservername = "localhost";
$dbusername = "YourDataBaseUserName";
$dbpassword = "YourPassword12345";

// Create a new connection object
$dbconnection = new mysqli($dbservername, $
dbusername, $ dbpassword);

// Check if connection was successful
if ($dbconnection->connect_error) {
    die("Connection failed/error: " . $dbconnection-
>connect_error);
}
```

```
echo "Connected successfully to database";
?>
```

In this example, you are using PHP's MySQLi to connect to your database. If you are going to test the code in the server that you installed in your computer, use localhost for your database's server name.

By the way, to prevent hackers on any random internet surfers to edit or access your databases, your MySQL server will require you to set a username and password. Every time you connect to it, you will need to include it to the parameters of the mysqli object.

In the example, you have created an object under the mysqli class. All the information that the server will send to you will be accessible in this object.

The third block of code is used to check if your connection request encountered any trouble. As you can see, the if statement is checking whether the connect_error property of the object $dbconnection contains a value. If it does, the code will be terminated and return an error message.

On the other hand, if the connect_error is null, the code will proceed and echo a message that will tell the user that the connection was successful.

Closing a connection

To close a mysqli object's connection, just invoke its close() method. For example:

```
$dbconnection->close();
```

Creating a new MySQL Database

```
<?php
$dbservername = "localhost";
$dbusername = "YourDataBaseUserName";
$dbpassword = "YourPassword12345";
```

```
// Create a new connection object
$dbconnection = new mysqli($dbservername, $ dbusername, $ dbpassword);

// Check if connection was successful
if ($dbconnection->connect_error) {
    die("Connection failed/error: " . $dbconnection->connect_error);
}


// Creating a Database

$dbSQL = "CREATE DATABASE YourDatabaseName";

if ($dbconnection->query($dbSQL) === TRUE) {

    echo "YourDatabaseName was created.";

}

else {

    echo "An error was encountered while creating your database: " . $dbconnection->error;

}

$dbconnection->close();
?>
```

Before you request a database to be created, you must connect to your MySQL server first. Once you establish a connection, you will need to tell your server to create a database by sending an SQL query.

The $dbSQL variable was created to hold the query string that you will send. You do not need to do this, but creating a variable for your queries is good practice since it will make your code more readable. If you did not create a variable holder for your SQL, you can still create a database by:

$dbconnection->query("CREATE DATABASE YourDatabaseName")

The if statement was used to both execute the query method of $dbconnection and to check if your server will be able to do it. If it does, it will return a value of TRUE. The if statement will inform you that you were able to create your database.

On the other hand, if it returns false or an error instead, the example code will return a message together with the error.

Once the database was created, the connection was closed.

Interacting with a Database

Once you create a database, you can now send SQL queries and do some operations in it. Before you do that, you need to connect to the server and then specify the name of the database, which you want to interact with, in the parameters of the mysqli class when creating a mysqli object. For example:

```
<?php
$dbservername = "localhost";
$dbusername = "YourDataBaseUserName";
$dbpassword = "YourPassword12345";

$dbname = "sample"

// Create a new connection object
$dbconnection = new mysqli($dbservername, $
dbusername, $ dbpassword, $sample);

// Check if connection was successful
if ($dbconnection->connect_error) {
    die("Connection failed/error: " . $dbconnection-
>connect_error);
}
```

```
echo "Connected successfully to database";
?>
```

phpMyAdmin

In case you do not want to rely on code to create and manage your databases, you can use the phpMyAdmin tool. Instead of relying on sending SQL queries, you will be given a user interface that is easier to use and reduces the chances of error since you do not need to type SQL and create typos. Think of it as Microsoft Access with a different interface.

The tool will also allow you to enter SQL if you want to and it will provide you with the SQL queries that it has used to perform the requests you make. Due to that, this tool will help you get more familiar with SQL. And the best thing about it is that it is free.

On the other hand, you can use phpMyAdmin to check the changes you made to the database while you are studying MySQL. If you do that, you will be able to debug faster since you do not need to redisplay or create a code for checking the contents of your database using PHP.

Conclusion

Thank you again for purchasing this book!

I hope this book was able to help you to master the fundamentals of MySQL programming.

The next step is to learn more about:

- Advanced SQL Statements and Clauses
- Attributes
- The MySQLi Class
- PHP Data Object
- Security Measures in MySQL
- Importing and Exporting MySQL Databases
- Different Applications of MySQL

Those topics will advance your MySQL programming skills. Well, even with the things you have learned here, you will already be capable of doing great things. With the knowledge you have, you can already create an online chat application, social network site, and online games!

That is no exaggeration. If you do not believe that, well, check out the sample codes that experts share on the web. You will be surprised how simple their codes are.

Finally, if you enjoyed this book, please take the time to share your thoughts and post a review on Amazon. We do our best to reach out to readers and provide the best value we can. Your positive review will help us achieve that. It'd be greatly appreciated!

Thank you and good luck!

Check Out My Other Books

Below you'll find some of my other popular books that are popular on Amazon and Kindle as well. Simply click on the links below to check them out. Alternatively, you can visit my author page on Amazon to see other work done by me.

Android Programming in a Day

Python Programming in a Day

C Programming Success in a Day

C Programming Professional Made Easy

JavaScript Programming Made Easy

PHP Programming Professional Made Easy

C ++ Programming Success in a Day

Windows 8 Tips for Beginners

HTML Professional Programming Made Easy

Programming Box Set #87: Facebook Social Power & MySQL Programming Professional Made Easy

If the links do not work, for whatever reason, you can simply search for these titles on the Amazon website to find them.